Pom Pom book box kit

Author

Katy Godbeer

Published by

Avec UK

Introduction

Crafty Monsters are scary, spooky, fluffy, sweet and a little bit naughty!

With mischievous monsters, cute creatures and adorable animals, there are plenty of fun friends to create to help you with your homework, watch over you while you craft or just keep you company! Using fun to make fuzzy pom poms they are quick and easy to create and just waiting for you to bring to life!

how to make a pom pom

step 1

Sandwich approximately 30cm of yarn between the two matching parts of the pom pom maker.

6

Wind yarn around both halves until you have a nice chunky covering of yarn, being careful not to trap the free ends of the yarn.

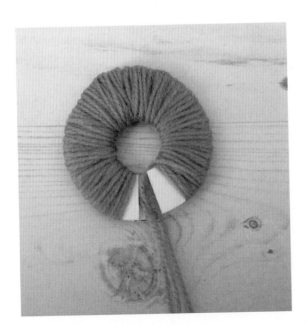

Tie a knot in the free ends of the yarn.

step 4

Insert the ends of scissors into the gap between the templates and cut all the way around the edge of the template discs tightening the knot gradually as you cut.

step 5

Remove the discs and fluff up the pom pom. Trim the yarn to give a nice even pom pom.

tips

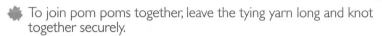

🌸 To join pom poms together, leave the tying yarn long and knot together securely.

🌸 To make a two coloured pom pom simply wind part of the discs in two different colours.

To make a multi-coloured pom pom wind with several colours of yarn at once.

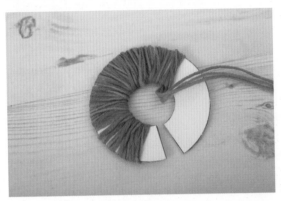

To make the felt parts – use tracing paper to trace the templates. Place onto the felt and cut around the edges. Use PVA glue to attach.

friendly monsters

*Make these fun little characters in your favourite colours –
choose just one colour or make a multicolour monster for even
more fun!*

little monster

🌸 Make a small pom pom and trim
neatly.

🌸 Make a mouth from felt using the
template. Separate the strands of
the pom pom to leave a mouth
shaped space. Fold the mouth in
half and use plenty of PVA glue
to attach to the pom pom.
Allow to dry.

🌸 Fold a chenille stem to make arms
and coil another to make a set of
feet. Glue to the monster with
PVA glue.

🌸 Add googly eyes to finish.

big monster

❀ Make a multi colour pom pom with three colours of yarn.

❀ Make a set of feet using the template and glue to the bottom of the monster.

❀ Make a mouth from felt using the template. Separate the strands of the pom pom to leave a mouth shaped space. Fold the mouth in half and use plenty of PVA glue to attach to the pom pom. Allow to dry.

🌸 Fold a chenille stem in half and coil both ends to make eye stalks – glue in place and add googly eyes using PVA glue.

templates

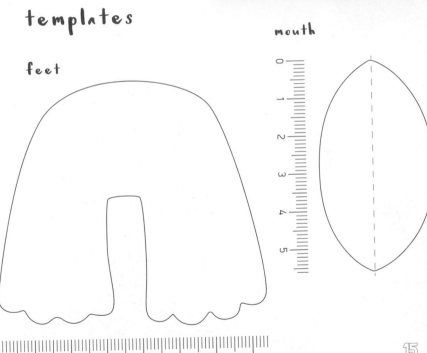

mouth

feet

Spooky friends

Perfect for Halloween these frighteningly fun friends are just the ticket for some scary adventures!

halloween bat

🌸 Make a small pom pom using black yarn. Trim neatly.

🌸 Trim 4 wing shapes from black felt. Glue pairs of the wings together to make them more stiff. You might like to stitch around the edge of the wings to add more detail. Glue either side of the bat using PVA glue.

🌸 Cut two ear shapes and pinch each at the base to shape them. Glue at the top of the pom pom.

🌸 Add googly eyes using PVA glue.

halloween ghost

🌸 Wrap white wool around your hand. Remove and knot with more yarn on one side only.

🌸 Cut the yarn on the opposite side

🌸 Loosely knot more yarn around the bunch of wool to make the head of the ghost.

🌸 Cut out the features of the ghost using the templates. Glue in place with PVA glue.

scary eyeballs

🌸 Use the smaller pom pom maker and wind on a small amount of black wool – this makes the pupil of the eye.

🌸 Cover the whole of the black section with blue, green or brown wool – this makes the iris of the eye.

🌸 Cover the whole of the rest of the pom pom maker with white wool to make up the rest of the eye.

🌸 Finish your pom pom as usual and trim neatly.

why not try?

- A scary spider
- A fun pumpkin
- Creepy skulls
- A cute cat

templates

ears

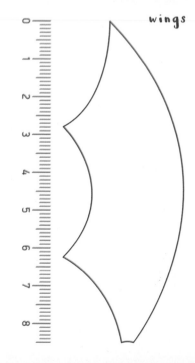

wings

hop to it!

frog

* Make a large green pom pom and leave the tying strands long.

* Wind green wool around 3 fingers. Carefully remove and knot around all the layers with more yarn. Trim neatly. Make a second matching mini pom pom and leave the tying strands long.

* Knot the two small pom poms together using one end of the tying strands from each pom pom.

* Use the remaining strands and the strands on the larger pom pom to tie the small pom poms to the larger pom pom.

* Make a mouth from felt using the template. Separate the strands of the large pom pom to leave a mouth shaped space. Fold the mouth in half and use plenty of PVA glue to attach to the pom pom. Allow to dry.

- Use the template to cut two feet shapes. Glue onto the base of the large pom pom.

- Add googly eyes using PVA glue.

templates

mouth

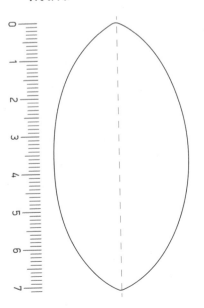

feet

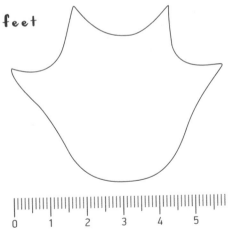

get the buzz!

Make this adorable stripy bumblebee, perfect for summer days in the garden!

bee

🌸 Make a smaller pom pom using black yarn.

🌸 Use the large pom pom maker and apply stripes of yellow and black yarn as shown in the picture. Tie off as usual and trim neatly.

* Make a small pom pom using black yarn and join together.

* Fold a black chenille stem in half and coil either end to make antenna.

- Cut 4 wings using the template – glue two pairs together to make them more stiff and glue to the bee in between the two pom poms.

- Finish with a pair of googly eyes.

templates

wings

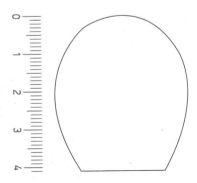

ewe-nique

Ewe'll just love this woolly pair. Why not make a whole flock?

sheep

* Make a large or small pom pom using white yarn.

* Tie off and trim neatly.

* Use the template to cut a face and glue to the top of the pom pom.

* Fold black chenille stems to make arms and legs and use PVA glue to add to the sheep.

❋ Finish with a pair
of googly eyes.

templates

sheep head

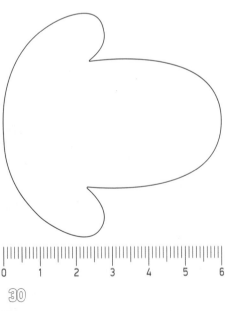

lamb head

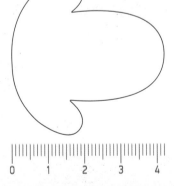

Penny the piggy

Who could resist this cute piggy friend?

piggy

🌸 Make large and small pom poms using pink yarn – leave the tying strands long.

🌸 Join the pom poms together and trim neatly.

🌸 Use chenille stems to create arms for your piggy.

- Use the templates to cut ears and a snout from pink felt and nostrils from white felt.

- Finish with a pair of googly eyes.

  You can make a piglet using the smaller pom pom and another wrapped around your fingers.

templates

outer nose

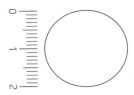

inner nose

ears

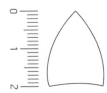

Counting your chickens

Make this eggstra cute clutch of chicks and mummy hen for Easter or just because!

hen

🌸 Make a small and a large pom pom using peach yarn. Join them together using the tying strands.

🌸 Trim the larger pom pom so that it has a flatter bottom and a more pointy part at the rear so that it resembles the shape of a chicken.

🌸 Use the templates to cut two of the comb shape and two of the wattles from red felt. Glue the combs together to make it stiffer. Glue in place.

* Cut wings and beak from orange felt and glue in place.

* Finish with a pair of googly eyes.

chicks

* Wind yellow wool around 2 fingers. Carefully remove and knot around all the layers with more yarn. Trim neatly.

* Finish with a pair of googly eyes and a tiny beak.

tip-

To make a hatching chick carefully chip away an empty egg shell to make a space to fit the chick inside. Wash thoroughly before inserting the chick into the shell.

hen comb

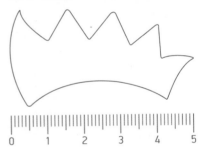

templates

hen wings

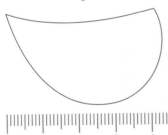

hen beak

chick beak

hen wattles

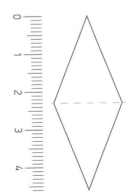

What a hoot

This wise pair would make a great gift for a student or teacher.

owl

- Make a small pom pom using beige and brown wool. First wind on two sections of beige wool as shown.

- Cover the beige sections with brown wool.

- Fill the rest of the pom pom with brown wool.

- Make a large pom pom for the owl's body – first wind on almost half of the pom pom using a strand of beige and a strand of brown yarn at the same time.

- Cover the two colour section and finish the rest of the pom pom with brown yarn.

- Finish and trim both pom poms - join together.

- Use the templates to cut two large wings, a large beak and two of the eye sections. Glue in place with PVA glue.

- Finish with a pair of googly eyes.

owlet

- Make a extra small pom pom by winding beige wool around 3 fingers. Carefully remove and knot around all the layers with more yarn. Trim neatly.

- Use the templates to make two small wings, an eye section and a small beak from felt. Glue in place using PVA glue

- Finish with a pair of googly eyes.

templates

owlet eyes

owlet wings

owl wings

owlet beak

owl eyes

owl beak

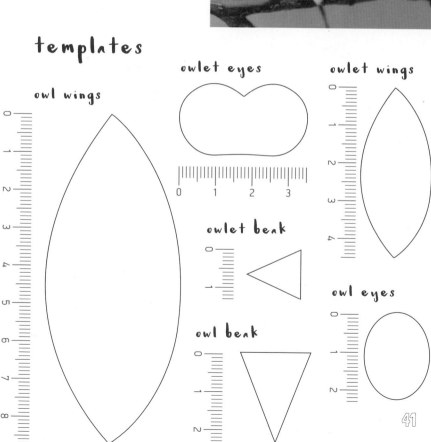

Something fishy

Make a cute watery scene with these fun fishy friends!

jellyfish

 Wrap magenta wool around your hand. Remove and knot with more yarn on one side only.

🌸 Cut the yarn on the opposite side to make a tassel shape. Leave the tying strands long.

🌸 Make a small pom pom in matching yarn. Finish and trim neatly.

🌸 Knot the pom pom to the long stranded tassel.

🌸 Finish with a pair of googly eyes.

fish

🌸 Wind sections of orange yarn onto the pom pom maker.

🌸 Wind white yarn into the spaces and over the orange sections.

🌸 Add further orange yarn on top of the sections of white yarn.

Finish and trim the
pom pom neatly.

Use the templates
to cut fins, a tail and
a mouth. Separate
the strands of the
pom pom to leave a
mouth shaped space.
Fold the mouth in
half and use plenty
of PVA glue to attach
to the pom pom. Add
the fins and tail.

Finish with a pair
of googly eyes.

templates

fins

mouth

dorsal fin

tail

45

About the author

Katy has worked in the crafting industry for more than a decade, creating, writing about and photographing all manner of creative endeavours, and while her Pug and Newfoundland dogs are definitely her first love, crafting comes a close second. From papercraft to sewing, soap making to upcycling, any craft is fair game for a cheeky dabble. These cute pom pom critters are a real childhood throwback and kids (and kids at heart) will be hard-pushed to resist them – her personal favourite is the chicken family!

Pom Pom book box kit

Author

Katy Godbeer

Published by

Avec UK

Manufactured by Avec Trade Ltd.
www.avecuk.com
For personal use only. Not for resale.

Designed in the UK
Produced responsibly in PRC for Avec UK